Oh
Yes He
Can

A Traveling Evangelist's Story
of God's Promises and Provisions

EVANGELIST WILBUR CONWAY

SAN DIEGO

OH YES HE CAN
Wilbur Conway
Published 2016
San Diego, CA
United States of America

If you would like to use material from the book (other than for review purposes), prior written permission must be obtained by contacting the author at P.O. Box 213, Higginsville, MO 64037

Unless otherwise noted, all Scriptures quotations are from the King James Version of the Bible.

ISBN-10 0-9909199-4-3
ISBN-13 978-0-9909199-4-0

CONTENTS

FOREWORD

In the Bible in Exodus 10:2, the Lord told Moses that He gave the Children of Israel the wonderful stories about how He hardened Pharaoh's heart and then delivered them from Pharaoh's wrath so that they could tell those stories to their children to make them know and love Him and identify His works. Likewise, the stories in this book are about the experiences that God gave my father when his heart was hardened. I'm sure that God wants to use them to pass the wisdom contained in them on to His children, grandchildren and future generations so that we all can love Him and identify His work in our lives. Just as the Children of Israel's stories are not just stories about them, my father's stories are not just about him; they are about God and the lessons that He wants to use them to teach.

As you read this book you will see that by the time my father was 19 years old he had made many more BIG mistakes than most individuals have made in their lifetime; from the trials and tribulations of my dad, and ones of my own. I have learned that doing the right thing is not always the easiest thing. I have also learned that being the person that one was meant to be is also not always the easiest accomplishment made. But, when your heart of hearts tells you to do or not to do something and/or leads you to establish yourself to be a certain person and/or live a certain way, one must dig down deep and congregate the strength to accomplish that task and/or be that person.

Can God fix our convoluted lives? Oh yes He can!!

In this book you will read that my father was more keen in his instinct ...he was sharper in his intuitions, his intuitiveness was more refined simply because it has been cultivated in the furnace of his afflictions. He had to learn how to survive in the midst of the hate, the disappointments, the hurt...as the complications were the clues and preparation of what God was about to do!

Can God do it? Oh yes he can!

You will learn that Faith is active, energetic; (Hope is us to our hope.) Trust is different from faith or hope. If you can trust something made by man, then you need to put your trust in God.

If you put your trust in God like that— then you have to understand that He has brought you into your season for such a time as this. God promises that He will open up the windows of heaven and will give you continued good success...

So laugh at the stories as we do now. . . and your laughter will lighten your heart and help to bring you to the understanding that no matter what you are experiencing in your life that if God brings you to it; He will bring you through it. Oh yes He can!

Love you much Dad,

Robin

DEDICATION

This book is dedicated to those who doubt and wonder whether or not God loves them and can deliver them.

A PROMISE

This book is my boast of God's unfailing grace and mercy as well as His ability to prove to me that He sees us all the same.

I know God brings us under conviction with His spirit and by acknowledging Him and repenting of our sins we can receive peace and freedom from spiritual and mental oppression. This is what God did for me.

My mother's, Myrtle Haynes-Conaway, and my stepfather's, William M. Conaway, (whose last name I carry minus the "a") religious backgrounds were Methodist and so I was baptized at the age of nine by Rev. Jordan of St. James AME. Church in Higginsville, Missouri. I had no idea what baptism meant so it did not bring about a change in my life.

It wasn't until I turned 18 years of age that I understood why I held such different facial features from my two younger sisters and why I was treated so differently by my step-dad and his side of the family. I was told that my real dad's last name was Young. Being an illegitimate child to my mom and step-dad who were not married at the time of my birth had a very negative impact on my life and self-esteem.

Once I found out everything, the reason for the treatment and other family issues became very clear. I became a very bitter 18 year old young man. The more I think of it, I really was a pretty confused kid before the age of 18. I believe that was the age that I became aware of the obvious.

Well God provided a way out of Higginsville, Mo. for me, and what I considered a very bad situation. The way out for me was the United States Navy.

Before I could leave Higginsville, Missouri, my mother went home to be with the Lord. It is my hope to see her again. Yes He Can!

I also spent a day in jail because I'd gotten a young girl pregnant. I didn't realize at that time that in all things God works for the good of those who love Him and who have been called according to His purpose.

I now understand that it was good for me to be afflicted and to experience tribulations. If I had not experienced these trying times, (some due to my actions and others out of my control) I would have never known the Glory of God. Thank you Lord for everything I went through!!

MY ESCAPE

By the end of the year I was fortunate enough to graduate from high school and enlist in the United States Navy. So much had transpired in such a short period of time; I had gotten myself in quite a mess! On my way to boot camp I made up my mind to never return to Higginsville. What I once considered home had become a place of suffering and shame. It was also a place where God had initially called me; a place where He would call me back to in the fullness of His time.

You see, although I had no understanding of the way God worked out His plan for one's life; He'd shown me snippets of His plan for my life in 1948 in

Higginsville, Missouri at the age of eleven. I just didn't understand the connection. Back then God had planted a seed of preaching in my heart. I would take my two younger sisters and have them act as my congregation. I used a little New Testament Bible that was given to me in school. One night while I was preaching to my sisters and my great aunt Sally, who happened to live right next door, my great aunt Sally was touched by the spirit of God and began to shout. Of course my sisters and I were quite amused by the reaction the preaching had caused. Aunt Sally shared her shouting experience with her niece and my Aunt Ruth who voiced her doubts of my ever becoming a preacher. I didn't realize that I was anointed but wasn't yet appointed.

Many times at parties I would joke or amuse people by pretending I was preaching. Recently I was preaching at one of my sister's churches and she had the task of introducing me. One of her statements referred back to a time when we played church in that old duplex house as kids. Finishing the statement she said "We are not playing anymore, thank God."

Once I was in the United States Navy, I became very eager to learn and quickly became a leader in whatever I strived to do. In boot camp you could earn petty officer stripes. There was no increase in pay status, of course, but you had a bit of authority over the rest of your company. I held the position of Master at Arms. I guess I don't have to tell you that I thoroughly abused my power.

Back in high school I had done a little boxing and in boot camp those skills came in handy. Recreational sports such as boxing were used to build competition between companies in boot camp. Boxing bouts were called "Smokers". I earned a great deal of respect by winning one of these boxing matches and I used it. All of my military career I never knew God as my Father nor Jesus Christ as my Savior and I was a total wild man.

OUT OF THE WORLD

In 1958, while stationed in Pensacola, Florida. I met a Catholic School girl named Corinne Marie Shumaker. It was the month of May. The same month my step-dad died. After the funeral, I returned to Pensacola and Corinne and I began to date steadily. It was a hot courtship and it was not long before we were in trouble. However, we thought we were in love at the time. It was only God, through His mercy and grace, who taught us how to truly love one another.

Corinne was pregnant with our first child and we believed we were ready for marriage. Neither one of us had a clue what marriage really was. I always thought to be a husband and father all I needed to do was provide a roof, food, and clothing. I thought that made me the "man of the house". I'd learned from my upbringing that if I was a good provider most of my responsibility was taken care of. Needless to say, this did not help our marriage relationship at all, because I felt after working and paying the bills I had a right to drink, run the streets chasing women, and gamble. I did whatever felt good and I felt that I was free to do so. After all, I was a man.

We struggled through 18 years of being married. Only when we received Jesus in our hearts as our Lord and personal Savior did we learn what it really meant to be husband and wife.

This understanding came after we attended our church, St. Stephen's Church Of God In Christ, where Bishop George D. McKinney was the pastor. We traveled to a married couples conference where the purpose of and Gods plan for Holy Matrimony were explained. The conference was hosted by San Francisco Christian Center. In one of the sessions, Bishop Donald Green prayed for me to receive the gift of salvation. I thank God for my gift of salvation and for the prayer that was graciously received by

Bishop Donald Green.

Corinne's family background was a little more stable than mine. Her Dad and Mom were in the home when she grew up. Her dad was a Baptist minister, and her mom sent her children to a Catholic School. Therefore, there was some positive structure to their growth as youth. I don't know enough facts to speak honestly about Corinne's childhood only what she and the rest of the family members shared with me over the years. Regardless of the both of our backgrounds neither one of us was prepared for what lay ahead of us. Under the best of family spiritual, parental standards and guidelines, marriages don't work out. It is two people working together to solve their problems. I should add here with the help of God who is the problem solver. Oh Yes He Can!

Now we were married, Karen our first born was here and we had no earthly idea of how to be parents. I must say that Corinne's family did help a lot at this time.

As I stated earlier I had no idea what it meant to be a Godly man, so not only was I miserable but I made many people around me the same.

The Navy gave me a certain amount of security. The benefits for myself and my family kept us independent of our families on both sides and it provided me with travel experience that helped me later on in my life.

Corinne and I went on to have three more children of our own and two of someone else's, and we truly love the two of them the same as our very own.

Upon completing 11 years, one month and 18 days in the Navy, I medically retired, as the result of losing an eye while in the service. However, traveling in the Navy had provided me with a desire to broaden my horizons, and once I was retired from the Navy I went back to school with an ambition to be a politician, not knowing that God had a call on my life that at that time I refused to accept.

God allowed me to gain employment at a government facility and to rise to a position that gave me a false sense of security. Going to college at the same time gave me enough education to make me think I had an edge on many of my peers. I had the

family, the house, the cars, the truck and the boat--
the American dream was mine. King Solomon said it
much better when he said "All is vanity" and truly
that is the American dream; it is empty without God.
After several attempts to find God on my own,
Corinne and I went to our first Marriage Conference,
of course I fought going and even after we arrived at
the site I still would not cooperate with the agenda.
Needless to say, this Marriage Conference is where
God brought me in out of the world and thanks be to
God I haven't gone back since. Of course that is not
to say I haven't looked back. I have only to realize
it's not for me. I had no understanding what it meant
to be a true Christian after being led in the sinner's
prayer at the conference by Rev. Donald Green of
the San Francisco Christian Center the host of the
conference.

I still had planned to go to a Ball in downtown San
Diego when Connie and I returned home from the
conference, and guess what? I did attend the ball.
Needless to say it was the worst time I ever had. It
was as though I didn't know how to dance or flirt

with the ladies, and my taste for alcohol totally left me.

So I left the dance early, went home, got up Sunday morning and went to church with my family and we lived happily ever after-yeah right!!

It was at St. Stephen COGIC that I totally publicly acknowledged Jesus Christ as my personal Savior, and I must state here and now that St. Stephens is and was a soul saving station if ever there was one.

After salvation, and being born again, comes the spiritual growth factor. I had been called at an early age and now I believe my spiritual growth went forward with great speed. I can relate to the Apostle Paul in a way, I was now 39 years of age, a non-believer and did not care about the Church or the people that attended them. By this time I had seen so many of my family members, friends and enemies playing Church as I did when I was a kid I just didn't believe God was real-BUT oh yes He is!! Also, by the time I was 39 I had delved into the horoscope religion on the college campus, I had looked at being a Muslim, and I had sat with a Buddhist section a couple of times and chanted and my brother-in-law had introduced me to transcendental meditation. What a Mighty God we serve.

Right after I received the gift of salvation, I worked for the government and felt like I would be on the job until retirement, not so. God had saved me and of course this was always a call that I resisted. Now it was confirmed time after time that I would be a minister of the gospel of Jesus Christ. At different times God would send someone to remind me that I was to be a preacher.

A PROMISE REALIZED

In February of 1980, when I had been ordained an Evangelist for four years, my wife came and shared with me that she had a vision that I was coming off the job and once again I took it lightly. Being very materialistic I had always wanted the very best for me and my family- the big house, several cars, a boat and all that goes with the American dream.

I believe God has a way of allowing you to taste the ways of the world as He did with the apostle Paul and then bring you in to serve Him. So He allowed me to tarry in the ways of the world and we enjoyed the big house with five bed rooms, three baths, a loft master bedroom with a huge walk- in closet, decks on both sides of the master bedroom overlooking a lake at the foot of a mountain, a Buick, a fifteen passenger van, and a 14-foot boat. I could go on and on with all the countless things too numerous to list. The point that I'm trying to make is that I feel God wanted me to see what it was like to have the temporal things in this life so I would not yearn for or put them ahead of the eternal and spiritual things, which are His. Oh Yes He Can!

In June of 1980 I became sick and could not determine in my mind what was going on with me. I was listless with no energy and no desire to get up to go to work or to do anything else. I lay in bed for two days before I decided to challenge God in prayer. Did I not have that right as an ordained Evangelist and living as righteously as I knew how at the time?

I am thinking God had a bit of a laugh because it not only took two days of me being sick for me to decide to pray, but when I did pray it was to question Him about my problem.

I prayed, "Lord why am I feeling this way? After all I am a true man of God; one of your Evangelists in the field." Some answers to prayers come quickly, some, not so quickly. I was barely finished before I received my answer to that prayer. First, I remembered my wife telling me I would be coming off the job soon. Then the quiet, still voice came to me again. I'd heard it a couple times before and that time I knew it was Him. It shocked me into submission when I heard Him speak and I realized in that moment I had felt that because I had become an ordained Christian Evangelist I was an outstanding servant of God while really only serving self and family.

I finally prayed to God my submission prayer, Dear Lord, You don't have to kill me I will resign and go in the ministry full-time.

My supervisor, co-workers and friends thought I had lost my mind when I submitted my resignation. One of my friends asked if there was so much money in preaching that I could keep my family going with the income. I told them I didn't know, but that I would have to trust God to take care of us. Oh yes He can!

From the day I resigned in September of 1980 until today God has paid the bills. So many times God stepped in and paid bills for me and my family.

I was hired by our church as church administrator, and what an education I got. I found out that all I had learned in school, the military and the position in the government had been a piece of cake.

Up to that point I thought I was very intelligent because God blessed me to be pretty successful in my efforts to obtain the American dream. I soon realized spiritual things came differently than the material things. I was re-educated in the things of God.

While working as the Church administrator, I took on a job as black history teacher in the Christian School and what a joyful experience that was. Teaching youth was very fulfilling and I understood the scripture and God's concept of training up a child in the way he should go. A-men!

ZEALOUS

The job of Church administrator was one of the greatest spiritual lessons in all my 30 years of Christian experiences. Boy, was I ever the trouble maker, I brought all my government training to the table and was that an exercise in faith? While my family lived in a big house and both my wife and I were gainfully employed I couldn't have understood trusting in God for everything. After my wife left her full-time job our faith in God became a true factor in our lives. I had some hospital, jail, and street ministries, however, I had not drifted out too far from home base. From time to time our pastor sent us to churches to fill in for him and other pastors would call on me to come and bring the word of God to their congregations, but I knew there was a lot more to being an evangelist than what I was about doing.

In prayer one morning God gave me a vision of a ministry. He gave me the name and the fact that it was to be a team effort. Thus the Jesus Evangelistic Team in Service Inc. (JET-IS INC) was born. The 'Just shall live by faith' was becoming a reality for this man of God. God did it. Oh yes He can!

Jesus said in the book of Acts the first Chapter that "But ye shall receive power, after that the Holy Ghost is come upon you: and ye shall be witnesses unto me both in Jerusalem, and in all Judaea, and in Samaria, and unto the uttermost part of the earth." Well, needless to say we started in the uttermost part of the world. I can't tell you even now that we have arrived at getting it in the order that Jesus gave it to us, but we are working on it. We should have started at home (Jerusalem), but God looks after His own even when we get ahead of Him. It can be frustrating as well as a learning experience, but God promises He will never leave us nor forsake us. This even goes for those times that you move with so much zealousness that you arrive before God has you prepared to. The road is rockier than if God goes ahead of you and you follow. For a fact, if He God had not been with me I would have surely shipwrecked a long time ago.

I remember telling Bishop Cleveland how zealous many of my brothers in the ministry were at the time and he responded to me "Son, pray that God protects them and the devil doesn't beat all the zeal out of them and they backslide." God can and will protect us during those zealous periods in our walk with Him. Oh Yes He Can!

A LEAP OF FAITH

That's what God has done for me. He has kept this zealous Evangelist from being beaten into submission by the enemy. The Jet-Is Inc. has truly been an act of faith in God and He has proven to be faithful to the vision He has given me.

Not knowing where to start after incorporating the ministry as a tax exempt Christian ministry, I just took a leap of faith and began to travel after much prayer and fasting. With little or no contacts, just a few supporters, little money, and a new dodge van my family and I were on the road. Oh yes He Can!

God worked many miracles which I'm going to share with you hoping that it will build your faith in Him as it did for me and so many others.

My wife Corinne, our daughters Karen, Janine,

Sandra, Robin, and our son Ronald traveled from San Diego CA. to Pensacola FL. God opened doors for ministry with the help of Pastor Elder Young, who God elevated to Bishop in the Church Of God In Christ.

He allowed us to minister in several of his churches in the Pensacola Florida. area. He also took me to several other churches he ministered to in the nearby state of Alabama.

Needless to say his hospitality, love and trust helped the team fulfill its first mission in that area of the vineyard. Of course there were other churches and Pastors, after hearing of our ministry, who opened up their doors for us to minister.

Bishop John Young, Rev. R. W. Wells, Rev. Coker, Bishop Banks and Pastor Bums were only a few. From the first mission until today God proved Himself faithful. He took us across this country and into foreign countries, sometimes together as a team and other times it was just He and me. Oh yes He can!

With the help of our San Diego Pastor, Dr. George D. McKinney, now a Bishop in the Church Of God In Christ, and many of our brothers and sisters in St. Stephen COGIC, the Ministry grew into what it is today.

Before leaving our home and totally launching out on our own we received a great deal of teaching and training at St. Stephen's. There were several ministries available for us to learn about our vocation right on site.

God proved Himself faithful in so many ways, both then and now. One was the miracles he worked out in my life personally and for others we have ministered to.

I believe that God proves to his people that He can and will work in their lives. It is done in ways that not only give them hope but also allow others to witness the blessing.

The very first time I became aware of God's power working in and through the ministry He gave me, was in regards to the home we purchased while Corinne and I were still employed. Once we resigned from our jobs our income of around $80,000 a year went to between $800.00 and $1,000.00 a month. Through this He proved his word to me that the 'Just shall live by faith'. Our home (house), after three years of not making any mortgage payments, was in the 'pay today or be evicted' stage. While running revival services in Denver Colorado, my wife got a call from the Veterans Administration Office telling her that we needed be out of the house by the end of the month which was February of 1983. When I called home from Denver she shared the information with me. I tried to comfort her by telling her that I would take care of the matter when I got home even though I had no idea what I would do. While in the revival services God did a marvelous work in delivering a homosexual from his lifestyle. Many others in attendance shared their testimonies of healings and deliverance.

When after a week in Denver, I arrived back at home. I prayed to God for help with the call I was making to the V.A. and He did. The V.A. officer said to me "Mr. Conway, we want you and your family

out of the house at the end of this month, February."
I said, "Sir there is no way I can move this month."
He responded to me and asked me, "When can you move then?"
I clearly heard a voice say, "In the month of May." The officer replied stating, "Mr. Conway be out the house in May or we will be there to evict you off of the property." I thanked God and began to pray for a place to move to. Shortly after that there came a knock at the door, it was a property management owner by the name of Wilmer Cooks. He stated that I had been recommended to him. He thought I would make a good site manager and he had a job for me. I told him I had a job. I was an evangelist. He asked, "What if the job came with a new town house apartment as a part of my salary?"
I asked when all this would take place and he told me the construction on the townhouses would be completed in May, but he would put me on payroll and started my training on the construction site right away.
Prior to moving I received a request to travel to San

Bernardino, California. to run a revival service. I got another phone call from my former home in Higginsville Mo. stating that my Uncle Alfred, who had had a hand in raising me, was sick unto death. While preparing to get to Missouri the Holy Spirit spoke to me saying "Let the dead bury the dead." I shared that with my wife and she confirmed the same, stating that He had spoken the same words to her so I knew that my visit to my uncle would have to wait.

I went to San Bernardino and ran the revival. On the very first night, while I was ministering, a young Native American girl came in the church, made her way into the pulpit area and sat down. As the church officials rushed to get her I said to leave her alone and continued the message. Afterwards I beckoned for my wife to come and the two of us ministered to the young girl. She accepted Jesus Christ as her Savior and was present in every service for the rest of the week.

On the way to Higginsville, my wife and I drove past two ladies parked on the side of the highway attempting to change a tire. After going a mile the Holy Spirit spoke to me and said "Go back and assist those women and change that tire. "I told my wife I needed to go back and help the two women we just passed. Corinne said, "I wondered why you continued to drive past them." It was a few more miles before we found an exit and overpass going back to where they were located. When I got even with their car going west there was no turnout for me to get over to them on eastbound side of the freeway. After a very short prayer I left the side of road and went down a ravine. There were very steep hills on both sides. It seemed like it took a long time to reach the highway. Thanks be to God we were able to reach them.

After talking to them for a few minutes they shared that they were on their way to the hospital. The older lady had terminal cancer and neither of them were able to change the flat tire on the car.

While my wife ministered to them in our van I changed the tire. We prayed for them and I gave them a card of the ministry and again we were on our way to Missouri.

God kept my uncle until my wife and I arrived in Higginsville. We ministered for two and half days, the third night he went home to be with the lord. I was blessed to bring the message at the funeral service of my Uncle Alfred.

After a week in Missouri, we were on our way back to our home in San Diego and my wife said to me, "I sure hate to return to all those bills that we are going to face there at the house." At once the Holy Spirit told me to let my wife know she should not worry.

The bills would be taken care of. Can our God take care of our bills? Oh Yes He Can!

Here is proof that "The Just shall live by Faith." When we arrived back home in San Diego we were indeed met by a hand full of bills. I took them from our son Ronald, went upstairs to our bedroom and fell on my knees and prayed.

Lord You said You would take care of these, they are your bills. Amen! I went to bed and slept until the next morning. When I got up I went through the mail I figured was all bills. However, there was a letter in the mail from Oklahoma. I opened it to find a letter address to me from the husband of the senior woman we had helped by the side of the road in Missouri. He stated that his wife had gone to heaven. She had told him many times over the years past that God would always send help in the present time of trouble. She considered us the help God sent in that time of her need. He had placed a check in the letter that then helped us in our time trouble at that moment. Thank you Lord!

Further proof would be the time I took a team across country to minister where ever God opened a door. We were on the road approximately three weeks, sleeping in the van, in homes and churches. God wrought healings, deliverances, salvation and testimonies the likes I had never witnessed before. It was an awesome learning experience!

After a spiritual service one night I thought it was high time we ate a full course meal at a real restaurant. I failed to take the time to look at the amount of the offering we had received. I just told everyone on the team to order what they wanted to eat. It was six of us. At the close of meal and fellowshipping I finally look at the offering. It was only $11.00 total.

I prayed a very short prayer "Help Lord, Amen!" I gave my wife the keys to the van and sent her and the rest of the team outside to keep them from suffering any embarrassment just in case there was trouble that I may have caused. But God.

I approached the cashier and handed her the check without looking at it. She said "That will be $11.00 please." I gave her the $11.00 in the envelope and I hit the door running. I haven't stopped yet.

A-men!

When we got back home to San Diego we were once again confronted with a hand full of bills to pay. What a miracle God did this time.

After being on the road such a long time I told my wife I was going to bed. I needed to really rest and told her I would go to the credit union in the morning where I figured I had about $60.00 in our account.

I thought that I would buy some food for the house and that would be it for a while. However, when I got to the Credit Union I was told by cashier that I had $1,700.00 in my account. I prayed to God that if that was my money to let it be there the next day. The next day I decide to go to a different branch of the Credit Union and checked again. Sure enough the $1,700.00 was there and I rejoiced as I paid the bills. Hallelujah. Amen

I have learned that God is faithful and "He who has begun a good work in You will perform it until the day of Jesus Christ."

While ministering at a conference in San Diego, California, I made a presentation on marriage and family the way God had established it. The presentation opened a door for me minister to students at Irvine College in Los Angeles, California. The Lord also opened a door for me to minister to a men's group at a large Church in Seattle, Washington as well as Tacoma, Washington.

While at the conference in Seattle, the Holy Spirit spoke to a young man who asked me where my book was. I confessed I had never written one and took his question as a compliment. He looked me in the eye and said it was not fair for me to share so much knowledge then leave without any follow up and a book would be helpful for the ministry.

A couple months later, while at a service at our home church, a prophet by the last name of Hunt called me. He said, "I've been watching you and I can see that you are a thinker. Get going with the book."

A WORD FOR HIS PEOPLE

A year later, while ministering at a Church in Pensacola, Florida the pastor introduced me to a local minister who upon hearing my name said to me "I read your book."

I had a hard time convincing him that I had not written a book, however after that little episode I figured I had better get busy. I tried to write long hand, that did not work. I tried putting it on tape, that did not work. God showed me a computer on a television infomercial. After watching it I thought I could sit down before a monitor and work on a book. There were a couple of problems with this idea; first, I did not own a computer and second, I did not know how to use one either. I shared this one day with a friend named Ben Gallup. He asked me if I wanted to learn how to use a computer because one of the local colleges he worked for was trading out their old computers for new ones. They were also giving computer lessons and I could sit in the class. Look at God! I was on my way to becoming computer savvy, thank You Lord.

In the meantime, while I still needed a computer for myself, my cousin Aaron Haynes went and bought me a new top of the line computer and printer. I know that was God and I give Him all the praise and Glory, my God can and He will! Oh yes He can!

When God knows we have a word for his people He goes to great measures to see that it comes to pass.

After this, God gave me the title of the book and a year later the book "Man Hood God's Style" was completed and in another year it was published and is on the market today.

God is leading me in prayer and fasting towards a vision that I would like to share with you briefly in this book, believing that this too shall come to pass. There are so many men incarcerated in this country's prison. Many are in prison for crimes committed, however, others are in there doing time because of mandatory sentencing laws. This means many terms being served by prisoners are dictated by a law and the judges have no judgment of the cases before them. So many prisons are full of men and women who are nonviolent and were productive citizens but made a bad choice. A first time violator can find him or herself facing 10 to 15 years for half a pound of cocaine in his possession. In many states some government officials are trying to get such laws changed. In the meantime, healthy, young and intelligent men and women are just being housed at the taxpayers' expense. I believe God has once again given me an opportunity to prove His love for people by opening these prison doors. I am looking forward to this assignment.

The ministry God gave me, Jesus Evangelistic Team In Service. (JET-IS INC.), established in 1980, has partnered up with several other Faith Based Organizations to form a Coalition to work with inmates and ex-offenders. The ministry is to transition the men and women from incarceration back into the community as productive citizens. Has God performed this task for these His children? Yes He has. As Christians, true followers of God must believe He can and He will do all things we ask of Him according to His will.

Writing this book about the things He has done for me has reaffirmed my beliefs. I have never been more sure that all things are possible with God.

Oh Yes He can!

Oh Yes He Can